Yummy
Little
Cookbook

Rebecca Gilpin and Catherine Atkinson

Designed by Non Taylor and Amanda Gulliver
Illustrated by Non Taylor, Molly Sage, Kim Lane and Sue Stitt
Photographs by Howard Allman
Cover design by Erica Harrison
Edited by Fiona Watt

Contents

3   Chocolates & Sweets
33   Yummy things for Christmas
65   Delicious treats for Easter

05037123

CHOCOLATES & SWEETS

4	Sweethearts	20	Marshmallow crunch
6	Tropical fruit cups	22	Creamy fondants
8	Creamy coconut ice	24	Orange and lemon creams
10	Chocolate truffles	26	Magic marshmallow fudge
12	Chocolate-dipped fruit	28	Chocolate crunchies
14	Mini florentines	30	Wrapping ideas
16	Chocolate swirls	32	Sparkling gift tags
18	Chocolate bugs		

Beside each ingredients list, you can find out how long the chocolates and sweets will keep. If you give them as a present, make sure you also tell the person you are giving them to. In lots of the recipes, you will use teaspoons and tablespoons for measuring. Use measuring spoons if you have them, as they give you exactly the amount you need.

Sweethearts

To make about 30 sweethearts, you will need:

50g (2oz) icing sugar
50g (2oz) caster sugar
100g (4oz) ground almonds*
100g (4oz) full-fat sweetened condensed milk
red food dye
one small and one very small heart-shaped cutter
a baking sheet lined with baking parchment

These sweets need to be eaten within four days.

1. Sift the icing sugar into a large bowl. Add the caster sugar and ground almonds and stir them all together.

2. Make a hollow in the middle and add the condensed milk. Mix it in well, until the mixture is completely smooth.

3. Put half of the mixture into another bowl. Add two drops of red food dye. Mix in the dye really well, using your fingers.

4. Wrap both pieces of mixture in foodwrap. Put them in a fridge for 20 minutes. This makes them easier to roll out.

5. Sprinkle a little icing sugar onto a clean work surface. Roll out the pink piece, until it is about as thick as your little finger.

6. Use the larger cutter to cut out heart shapes. Cut them close together. Make the scraps into a ball, and roll it out.

* Don't give these to anyone who is allergic to nuts.

7. Cut out more hearts. Then, use the smaller cutter to cut out hearts from the middles of the big hearts.

8. Roll out the cream mixture, as before. Cut out large hearts. Then, cut small hearts out of their middles.

9. Gently press the small cream hearts into the big pink ones. Then, press the small pink hearts into the big cream ones.

10. Put the hearts onto the baking sheet. Leave them to dry and harden overnight. Store them in an airtight box.

Tropical fruit cups

To make 12 tropical fruit cups, you will need:

50g (2oz) sweetened dried pineapple
   or mango
  1 tablespoon of pineapple or orange juice
   100g (4oz) milk chocolate drops
    100g (4oz) white chocolate drops
     small foil or double thickness paper case

These chocolates need to be eaten within five days.

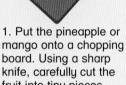

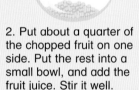

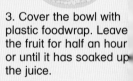

1. Put the pineapple or mango onto a chopping board. Using a sharp knife, carefully cut the fruit into tiny pieces.

2. Put about a quarter of the chopped fruit on one side. Put the rest into a small bowl, and add the fruit juice. Stir it well.

3. Cover the bowl with plastic foodwrap. Leave the fruit for half an hour or until it has soaked up the juice.

Do this while the fruit is soaking.

4. Pour about 3cm (1in) of water into a pan. Heat the pan until the water bubbles, then remove it from the heat.

5. Put the milk chocolate drops into a heatproof bowl. Wearing oven gloves, carefully put the bowl into the pan.

Wear ove gloves when yo lift the bowl ou

6. Stir the chocolate wit a wooden spoon until it has melted. Lift the bow out of the pan. Leave it to cool for three minutes

Spread the chocolate all the way up the sides.

7. Spread chocolate over the inside of the sweet cases with a teaspoon. Put them into a fridge for 20 minutes, until firm.

8. Spoon some of the soaked fruit into each chocolate case. Each case should be just over half full.

9. Melt the white chocolate in the same way that you melted the milk chocolate. Leave it to cool for three minutes.

10. Spoon the white chocolate over the fruit, so that it comes right to the top of the milk chocolate cases.

11. Put a piece of fruit on top of each chocolate. Chill them in a fridge for half an hour. Then, peel off the sweet cases.

12. Put the chocolates in an airtight container. Keep them in a fridge until you are ready to eat them.

Creamy coconut ice

To make 36 squares, you will need:

2 egg whites, mixed from dried egg white
(mix as directed on the packet)
450g (1lb) icing sugar, sifted
175g (6oz) desiccated coconut
4 teaspoons water
green food dye
a shallow 18cm (7in) square cake tin
greaseproof paper

Coconut ice
needs to be
eaten within
10 days.

1. Put the tin onto a piece of greaseproof paper. Draw around it and cut out the square, just inside the line.

2. Use a paper towel to wipe some oil onto the sides and bottom of the tin. Press in the paper square and wipe it too.

3. Put the egg whites into a large bowl. Stir them quickly with a fork for about a minute, until they are frothy.

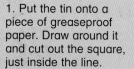

To make pink and white coconut ice, use red food dye instead of green.

8

4. Stir in two tablespoons of icing sugar. Add and stir in the rest of the icing sugar, a little at a time, until it is all mixed in.

5. Add the coconut and water and mix everything well. Spoon half of the mixture into the tin. Use your fingers to press it in.

6. Add a few drops of green food dye to the rest of the mixture. Stir the mixture until it is evenly coloured.

Smooth the top with the back of a spoon.

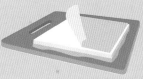

7. Spoon the green mixture on top of the white layer. Then, leave the tin in a cool place overnight.

8. Use a blunt knife to loosen the edges of the coconut ice. Turn it out onto a chopping board. Then, remove the paper.

9. Cut the coconut ice into 36 small squares. Leave them to harden for two hours. Keep them in an airtight container.

Chocolate truffles

To make about 10 truffles, you will need:

100g (4oz) milk chocolate drops
25g (1oz) butter
25g (1oz) icing sugar
50g (2oz) plain cake, crumbled into fine crumbs
4 tablespoons chocolate sugar strands
small paper cases

Chocolate truffles need to be eaten within five days.

Put chocolate truffles in boxes lined with tissue paper, to give as presents.

Wear oven gloves when you lift the bowl out.

1. Pour about 3cm (1in) of water into a pan. Heat the pan until the water bubbles, then remove it from the heat.

2. Put the chocolate drops and butter into a heatproof bowl. Wearing oven gloves, gently put the bowl into the pan.

3. Stir the chocolate and butter with a wooden spoon until they have melted. Carefully lift the bowl out of the water.

Use a teaspoon.

4. Sift the icing sugar through a sieve into the chocolate. Add the cake crumbs and stir until everything is mixed well.

5. Leave the chocolate mixture to cool in the bowl. Then, put the chocolate sugar strands onto a plate.

6. When the mixture is firm and thick, scoop up some with a teaspoon and put it into the chocolate strands.

Roll the spoonful to make a ball.

7. Using your fingers, roll the spoonful around until it is covered. Then, put it in a paper case. Make lots more truffles.

8. Put the truffles onto a plate. Put them in a fridge for 30 minutes. Keep them in an airtight container in the fridge.

Chocolate-dipped fruit

You will need:

450g (1lb) small strawberries
  with their stems left on
75g (3oz) milk chocolate drops
75g (3oz) white chocolate drops
baking parchment

The chocolate-dipped fruit needs to be eaten on the day you make it.

You can also dip other kinds of fruit in chocolate. Satsuma segments look pretty and taste delicious.

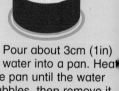

1. Put the strawberries in a sieve. Wash them under cold running water for a little time, to rinse them.

2. Gently pat them with a paper towel to remove most of the water. Then, spread them out on a plate. Leave them to dry.

3. Pour about 3cm (1in) of water into a pan. Heat the pan until the water bubbles, then remove it from the heat.

4. Put the milk chocolate drops into a heatproof bowl. Wearing oven gloves, carefully put the bowl into the pan.

5. Use a wooden spoon to stir the chocolate until it has melted. Using oven gloves, carefully lift the bowl out of the water.

6. Melt the white chocolate drops in the same way. Leave both bowls of chocolate to cool for two minutes.

. Dip a strawberry into
he melted chocolate.
he chocolate should
ome about halfway up
he strawberry.

Lift the strawberry out
nd let it drip over the
wl. Then, put it on a
ece of baking
rchment on a plate.

9. Dip the other
strawberries into the
chocolate. Then, put
them in a fridge for
about 20 minutes, to set.

10. Carefully peel the
strawberries off the
baking parchment, and
put them on a plate. Eat
them on the same day.

Mini florentines

To make about 18 mini florentines, you will need:

18 glacé cherries
18 unsalted halved walnuts or pecan nuts*
75g (3oz) plain chocolate drops
75g (3oz) white chocolate drops
a baking sheet lined with baking parchment

*Mini florentines
need to be eaten
within four days.*

*These mini
florentines are
topped with
pecan nuts and
glacé cherries.*

1. Put the cherries in a sieve. Rinse them under warm running water to remove the syrup. Dry them on a paper towel.

2. Put the cherries onto a chopping board. Chop each one carefully, using a sharp knife. Then, chop the nuts too.

3. Pour about 3cm (1in) of water into a pan. Heat the pan until the water bubbles, then remove it from the heat.

* Don't give these to anyone who is allergic to nuts.

4. Put the plain chocolate drops into a heatproof bowl. Wearing oven gloves, carefully put the bowl into the pan.

5. Stir the chocolate with a wooden spoon until it has melted. Using oven gloves, carefully lift the bowl out of the pan.

6. Spoon a teaspoon of melted chocolate onto the baking parchment. Make a neat circle, using the back of the spoon.

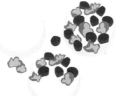

7. Gently press pieces of cherry and nut into the chocolate. Make more circles of chocolate and decorate them.

8. Then, melt the white chocolate drops. Make more circles with the chocolate and decorate them too.

9. Put the florentines in a fridge for half an hour. Then, carefully peel them off the paper. Keep them in an airtight container.

Chocolate swirls

To make about 25 chocolate swirls, you will need:

250g (9oz) icing sugar
half the white of a medium egg (3 teaspoons), mixed
    from dried egg white (mix as directed on the packet)
1 teaspoon of lemon juice
1 teaspoon of peppermint flavouring
1 tablespoon of cocoa powder
2 teaspoons boiling water
1 teaspoon of vanilla flavouring
a baking sheet covered in plastic foodwrap

Eat these within 10 days.

Pour the
mixture into
the hollow in
the sugar.

1. Sift the icing sugar
then put 100g (4oz) of it
into a large bowl. Make
a hollow in the middle
with a spoon.

2. Mix half of the egg
white with the lemon
juice and peppermint in
a small bowl. Pour the
mixture into the sugar.

3. Stir the mixture with a
blunt knife, then squeez
it with your fingers until
it is smooth. Wrap it in
plastic foodwrap.

If the mixture is a little dry, add a drop of water.

4. Sift the cocoa powder into a large bowl. Add the water and vanilla flavouring. Then, mix everything together well.

5. Add the rest of the egg white and stir it in. Add the rest of the icing sugar. Then, stir the mixture with a blunt knife.

6. Squeeze the mixture until it is smooth. Wrap it in foodwrap too. Put the two pieces in a fridge for 10 minutes.

7. Sprinkle a little icing sugar onto a clean work surface and a rolling pin. The icing sugar stops the mixture from sticking.

8. Roll out the white mixture into a rectangle 20cm x 15cm (8in x 6in). Do the same with the chocolate mixture.

9. Put the chocolate rectangle on top of the white one. Then, trim the edges with a knife to make them straight.

Roll the rectangle from one of the long edges.

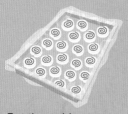

10. Tightly roll the rectangle into a sausage. Wrap it in foodwrap and put it in a fridge for about 10 minutes.

11. Using a sharp knife, carefully cut the sausage into slices which are about the thickness of your little finger.

12. Put the swirls onto the baking sheet. Leave them to harden overnight. Keep them in an airtight container.

Chocolate bugs

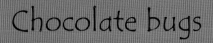

To make 10 bugs, you will need:

75g (3oz) plain chocolate drops
3 tablespoons golden syrup
75g (3oz) white chocolate drops

The bugs need to be eaten within a week.

Use a wooden spoon.

1. Pour about 3cm (1in) of water into a pan. Heat the pan until the water bubbles, then remove the pan from the heat.

2. Put the plain chocolate drops into a heatproof bowl. Using oven gloves, carefully put the bowl into the pan.

3. Stir the chocolate until it has melted. Wearing oven gloves, lift the bowl out of the pan. Leave it to cool for two minutes.

4. Stir in 1½ tablespoons of golden syrup until the mixture forms a thick paste which doesn't stick to the sides of the bowl.

5. Wrap the paste in plastic foodwrap. Then, melt the white chocolate and stir in the rest of the golden syrup, as before.

6. Wrap the white paste in plastic foodwrap. Chill both pieces of chocolate paste in a fridge for about an hour.

You could also
decorate the bugs
with stripes or
wiggly lines.

7. Take both pieces of chocolate paste out of the fridge. Leave them for about 10 minutes, to soften a little.

8. Cut the plain chocolate paste into six pieces. Wrap one piece in foodwrap again and put it on one side.

Smooth the edges of the oval shapes.

9. Make the other five pieces into oval shapes. Do the same with the white chocolate paste, to make 10 ovals altogether.

Make a shallow mark with the knife.

The second mark makes the wings.

10. To make a bug's head, gently press in the back of a blunt knife, a third of the way down a chocolate shape.

11. Make a second mark. Unwrap the last pieces of paste. Roll small balls to make eyes and spots. Press them onto the bug.

12. Put the bugs onto a plate. Cover them with plastic foodwrap. Keep them in a fridge until you are ready to eat them.

Marshmallow crunch

To make about 50 squares, you will need:

25g (1oz) glacé cherries
75g (3oz) puffed rice cereal
100g (4oz) pink and white marshmallows
25g (1oz) butter
a shallow 18cm (7in) square cake tin
greaseproof paper

*Marshmallow crunch needs
to be eaten within three days.*

1. Put the tin onto a piece of greaseproof paper. Draw around it and cut out the square, just inside the line.

2. Use a paper towel to wipe some oil onto the sides and bottom of the tin. Press in the paper square and wipe it too.

3. Put the glacé cherries on a chopping board. Carefully cut them into small pieces, using a sharp knife.

4. Put the puffed rice cereal and chopped cherries into a bowl. Mix them well with a wooden spoon.

5. Cut the marshmallows in half using a clean pair of scissors. Put the marshmallows and the butter into a large pan.

6. Gently heat the pan, stirring occasionally with a wooden spoon. Carry on until everything has just melted.

Use a wooden spoon.

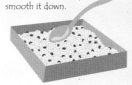

Push the mixture into the corners and smooth it down.

7. Remove the pan from the heat. Add the cereal mixture to the pan and stir everything until it is mixed together.

8. Spoon the mixture into the tin, and put it in a fridge for two hours. Then, loosen the edges with a blunt knife.

9. Turn the crunch out onto a board. Remove the paper. Cut the crunch into squares. Keep it in an airtight container.

Creamy fondants

To make about 40 creamy fondants, you will need:

250g (9oz) icing sugar
half the white of a small egg (2½ teaspoons), mixed
    from dried egg white (mix as directed on the packet)
1 teaspoon of vanilla flavouring
4 teaspoons of single cream
red and green food dye
small cutters
a baking sheet covered
    in plastic foodwrap

These sweets
need to be
eaten within
a week.

1. Sift the icing sugar through a sieve into a large bowl. Make a hole in the middle of the sugar with a spoon.

2. Mix the egg white, vanilla flavouring and single cream in a small bowl. Pour the mixture into the sugar.

3. Use a blunt knife to stir the mixture. Squeeze it between your fingers until it is smooth. Then, cut it into two halves.

4. Put each half into a separate bowl. Add a few drops of red food dye to one bowl and green dye to the other.

5. Mix in the red dye with your fingers. Add more icing sugar if the mixture is sticky. Mix the green dye into the other bowl.

6. Sprinkle a little icing sugar onto a clean work surface. Sprinkle some onto a rolling pin too, to stop the mixture sticking

Put creamy
fondants in boxes,
to give as presents.

Cut the shapes
close together.

7. Roll out the pink
mixture until it is about
as thick as your little
finger. Use cutters to cut
out lots of shapes.

8. Use a blunt knife to
lift the shapes onto the
baking sheet. Roll out
the green mixture and
cut out more shapes.

9. Put the shapes onto the
baking sheet. Leave them
for an hour to harden.
Keep them in an airtight
container in a fridge.

23

Orange and lemon creams

To make about 24 orange and lemon creams, you will need:

350g (12oz) icing sugar
1 small orange
half the white of a small egg (2½ teaspoons), mixed from dried egg white (mix as directed on the packet)
red and yellow food dye
1 lemon
a baking sheet lined with greaseproof paper

These sweets need to be eaten within 10 days.

Sweetie bags filled with orange and lemon creams make great presents. Find out how to make them on page 30

se the
small holes
on a grater.

. Sift half of the icing
sugar into one bowl and
half into another bowl.
Then, grate about half
of the skin of the orange.

Use a lemon
squeezer.

2. Cut the orange in half
and squeeze. Put the
juice into a bowl. Then,
put 1½ teaspoons of egg
white into another bowl.

3. Add the grated orange,
five teaspoons of juice, a
drop of red food dye and
two drops of yellow food
dye. Mix everything well.

Squeeze the mixture
until it is smooth.

. Add the mixture to
ne of the bowls of icing
sugar. Stir it with a blunt
knife, then squeeze it
with your fingers.

The marks make the
outsides look like
orange skin.

5. Sprinkle icing sugar
on a clean work surface.
Make about 12 orange
balls. Then, gently roll
them over a fine grater.

6. Grate about half of the
lemon's skin. Cut the
lemon in half. Squeeze
it and put five teaspoons
of the juice into a bowl.

. Add a few drops
of yellow food dye, the
grated lemon and 1½
teaspoons of egg white.
Mix everything together.

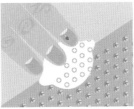

8. Mix the juice mixture
into the other bowl of
icing sugar, as before.
Make lemon shapes. Roll
them over a fine grater.

9. Put the sweets onto
the baking sheet. Leave
them for a few hours to
become firm. Keep them
in an airtight container.

Magic marshmallow fudge

To make 36 pieces, you will need:

450g (1lb) icing sugar, preferably unrefined
100g (4oz) white marshmallows
2 tablespoons milk
100g (4oz) unsalted butter
half a teaspoon of vanilla essence
a shallow 18cm (7in) square cake tin
greaseproof paper

The fudge needs to be eaten within a week.

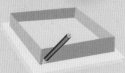

1. Put the tin onto a piece of greaseproof paper. Draw around it and cut out the square, just inside the line.

2. Use a paper towel to wipe some oil onto the sides and bottom of the tin. Press in the paper square and wipe it too.

3. Sift the icing sugar through a sieve into a large bowl. Make a sma hollow in the middle of the icing sugar.

4. Using scissors, cut the marshmallows in half and put them into a small pan. Add the milk, butter and vanilla essence.

5. Gently heat the mixture. Stir it every now and then with a wooden spoon until everything has melted.

6. Pour the mixture into the hollow in the icing sugar. Beat everything together with a spoon until it is smooth.

Smooth the fudge with the back of a spoon.

7. Put the fudge into the tin and push it into the corners. Use a spoon to make the top of the fudge as flat as you can.

Find out how to wrap pieces of fudge like this on page 31.

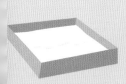

8. When the fudge is cool, put the tin in a fridge for about three hours, or until the fudge is firm.

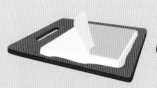

9. Use a blunt knife to loosen the edges of the fudge, then turn it out onto a chopping board. Remove the paper.

10. Cut the fudge into 36 pieces. Then, put it in a fridge for an hour to harden. Keep it in an airtight container.

Chocolate crunchies

To make about 25 chocolate crunchies, you will need:

75g (3oz) rich tea biscuits
50g (2oz) dried apricots
225g (8oz) white chocolate drops
4 tablespoons golden syrup
1 teaspoon of drinking chocolate
small paper cases

These chocolates
need to be eaten
within three day

1. Break the biscuits into tiny pieces and put them into a bowl. Cut the apricots into tiny pieces. Add them to the biscuits.

2. Pour about 3cm (1in) of water into a pan. Hea the pan until the water bubbles, then remove it from the heat.

3. Put the chocolate drops into a heatproof bowl. Wearing oven gloves, carefully put the bowl into the pan.

Wear over
gloves when yo
lift the bowl out

4. Stir the chocolate unti it has melted. Carefully li the bowl out of the wate Let the chocolate cool fc a minute.

You can also make these chocolates with plain or milk chocolate, and dust them with icing sugar.

5. Quickly stir in the golden syrup, then add the biscuits and apricots. Mix everything well with a wooden spoon.

6. Scoop up some of the mixture with a teaspoon. Using your hands, shape it into a ball and put it into a paper case.

7. Make lots more balls and put them onto a large plate. Put the sweets in a fridge for an hour, until they are firm.

8. Sift the drinking chocolate over the chocolate crunchies. Keep them in an airtight container in a fridge.

Wrapping ideas

Sweetie bags

1. Cut a square of thin cellophane. Then, lay five or six sweets or chocolates in the middle of the square.

2. Gather up the edges of the square around the sweets. Then, pull the edges together above the sweets, like this.

3. Cut a piece of parcel ribbon about 20cm (8in) long. Tie the ribbon tightly around the bag, above the sweets.

Pointed bags

The white line shows you where to cut.

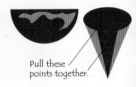

Pull these points together.

1. Cut a square of cellophane with sides 40cm (16in) long. Fold it in half, and then in half again.

2. Hold the corner where the folds join. Cut a quarter-circle, like this. Open out the cellophane shape. It is now a circle.

3. Cut the circle in half. Take one of the halves. Then, pull its two points towards each other until they meet.

4. Slide one of the points behind the other, to make a cone. Secure the cone with some pieces of sticky tape.

5. Half-fill the cone with sweets. Cut a piece of parcel ribbon 20cm (8in) long. Tie it around the cone, above the sweets.

Line a gift box with cellophane, then fill it with layers of sweets.

Wrapped sweets

Find out how to make sparkling gift tags on page 32.

1. Cut a square of thin cellophane that is bigger than the sweet. Put the sweet in the middle of the square.

2. Wrap the sweet in the piece of cellophane and tape it. Tie pieces of parcel ribbon around each end of the sweet.

Use a tiny piece of tape.

Sparkling gift tags

Ask someone to help you cut the potato.

1. Carefully cut a potato in half. Press the sharp edge of a star-shaped cookie cutter into the cut side of the potato.

2. Press the edge of the star cutter into some PVA glue. Press the cutter onto a piece of thin cardboard.

3. Before the glue dries, sprinkle it with lots of glitter. Shake off any extra glitter onto some scrap paper.

4. Cut around the star, a little way away from the glitter. Tape a piece of parcel ribbon to the back of the tag.

YUMMY THINGS FOR CHRISTMAS

34 Little Christmas trees
36 Coconut mice
38 Spicy Christmas stars
40 Creamy chocolate fudge
42 Crinkly Christmas pies
44 Painted biscuits
46 Starry jam tart
48 Peppermint creams

50 Shortbread
52 Fairy muffins
54 Shining star biscuits
56 Snowmen and presents
58 Iced gingerbread hearts
60 Christmas tree cakes
62 Wrapping ideas
64 Tags and ribbons

Little Christmas trees

To make 10 trees and 16 presents, you will need:
275g (9½oz) self-raising flour
225g (8oz) soft margarine
4 tablespoons milk
1 level teaspoon of baking powder
225g (8oz) caster sugar
2-3 drops vanilla essence
4 medium eggs

For the butter icing:
75g (3oz) butter, softened
175g (6oz) icing sugar
2 teaspoons lemon juice
food dyes

You could arrange the presents around the trees.

Heat the oven to 180°C, 350°F, gas mark 4, before you start.

Use a roasting tin.

Use a paper towel to wipe oil on the tin.

Use a wooden spoon.

1. Draw around a tin on greaseproof paper. Cut it out. Wipe oil inside the tin. Put the paper into the tin and oil the paper.

2. Sift the flour into a large mixing bowl. Add the margarine, milk, baking powder, sugar and vanilla essence.

3. Break the eggs into a small bowl. Beat them with a fork. Add them to the flour mixture. Beat everything together well.

Make trunks for the trees from chocolate bars or biscuits.

The cake should be springy when you press it.

4. Spoon the mixture into the tin. Smooth the top. Bake it in the oven for 40-45 minutes, until the middle is springy.

5. Leave the cake in the tin to cool, then lift it out. Put the butter into a bowl. Beat it with a wooden spoon until it is creamy.

6. Sift in the icing sugar and stir it in, a little at a time. Stir in the lemon juice. Put three-quarters of the icing in a bowl.

To make the colour stronger, add more dye, a drop at a time.

These will be the presents.

7. Mix in a little green food dye. Divide the rest of the icing into three bowls. Mix a drop of food dye into each one.

8. Cut a strip 7cm (3in) wide from one end of the cake. Cut it into 16 small squares. Cut the cake in half along its length.

9. Cut out ten triangles. Ice them with green icing. Ice the presents with the other icing. Press sweets onto the cakes.

Decorate the trees with sweets.

Coconut mice

To make about eight large mice, five medium mice and three baby mice, you will need:
250g (9oz) icing sugar, sifted
200g (8oz) tin of condensed milk
175g (7oz) desiccated coconut
red food dye
sweets for ears
silver cake-decorating balls
liquorice 'bootlaces'

1. Mix the icing sugar and the condensed milk together in a bowl. Mix in the coconut. Put the mixture into two bowls.

2. Add a few drops of red dye to each bowl and mix it in. Then add a few more drops of dye to one of the bowls.

For baby mice, use a teaspoon for the body.

3. Dip a clean tablespoon into some water and let it drip. Then, lift out a big spoonful of the mixture.

4. Pat the spoonful smooth on top. Turn the spoon over and put the shape onto a piece of plastic foodwrap.

5. Pinch a nose at the thinner end of the spoon shape. Then, add sweets for ears and silver balls for eyes.

6. Push a piece of liquorice under the shape, as a tail. Leave the mouse to harden on a plate. Make more mice.

Use a dessertspoon for a medium mouse.

Spicy Christmas stars

To make about 25 stars, you will need:
150g (6oz) self-raising flour
1 teaspoon of mild paprika
half a teaspoon of salt
75g (3oz) butter or margarine
75g (3oz) cheese, finely grated
1 egg and 1 tablespoon of milk, beaten together
a star-shaped cutter
a greased baking sheet

Heat the oven to 200°C, 400°F, gas mark 6,
before you start.

1. Sift the flour, paprika and salt through a sieve. Add the margarine or butter. Rub it with your fingers to make crumbs.

2. Leave a tablespoon of the grated cheese on a saucer. Add the rest of the cheese to the bowl and stir it in.

3. Put a tablespoon of the beaten egg and milk mixture into a cup. Mix the rest into the flour to make a dough.

Use a rolling pin.

Use a pastry brush.

4. Sprinkle flour onto a clean work surface. Roll out the dough, until it is slightly thinner than your little finger.

5. Use the cutter to cut out star shapes. Cut them close together. Make the scraps into a ball, and roll them out.

6. Cut out more stars. Brush the stars with the rest of the egg mixture, then sprinkle them with the rest of the cheese.

7. Put the stars onto the greased baking sheet. Bake them in the oven for eight to ten minutes, until they are golden.

These stars are delicious to eat when they are warm.

Creamy chocolate fudge

To make about 36 squares of fudge, you will need:
75g (3oz) full-fat cream cheese
350g (12oz) icing sugar
1 level tablespoon of cocoa powder
1 teaspoon of oil, for wiping
75g (3oz) plain chocolate drops
40g (1½oz) butter
a shallow 15cm (6in) square cake tin
greaseproof paper

Find out how to wrap pieces of fudge on page 62.

40

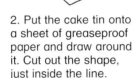

Use a pencil to draw around the tin.

1. Put the cream cheese into a bowl. Sift the icing sugar and cocoa through a sieve into the bowl too. Mix them together well.

2. Put the cake tin onto a sheet of greaseproof paper and draw around it. Cut out the shape, just inside the line.

3. Use a paper towel to wipe oil onto the sides and base of the tin. Press in the paper square and wipe it too.

4. Melt the chocolate and butter as in steps 1-3 on page 11. Then, stir in a tablespoon of the cream cheese mixture.

5. Pour the chocolate into the cheese mixture in the bowl. Beat them together with a spoon until they are creamy.

6. Spoon the mixture into the tin, and push it into the corners. Make the top of the fudge as flat as you can.

7. Smooth the top of the fudge with the back of a spoon. Put the tin in the fridge for two hours, or until the fudge is firm.

8. Use a blunt knife to loosen the edges of the fudge, then turn it out onto a large plate. Remove the paper.

9. Cut the fudge into lots of squares. Then, put the plate in the fridge for two hours, until the fudge is hard.

Crinkly Christmas pies

To make 12 pies, you will need:
4 eating apples
3 tablespoons orange juice or cold water
50g (2oz) dried cranberries or sultanas
2 teaspoons caster sugar
half a teaspoon of ground cinnamon
100g (4oz) filo pastry (about 6 sheets)
50g (2oz) butter
2 teaspoons icing sugar
a baking tray with shallow pans or 12-hole muffin tin

Heat the oven to 190°C, 375°F, gas mark 5, before you start.

You may need to ask someone to help you.

1. Peel the apples. Cut them into quarters and cut out the cores. Cut them into small pieces and put them in the pan.

Put the lid back on after you've stirred the apples.

2. Add the juice or water and put the pan on a very low heat. Cover it with a lid. Cook for 20 minutes, stirring often.

Stir the mixture often.

3. Stir in the fruit, caster sugar and cinnamon. Cook the mixture for about five minutes, then take it off the heat.

Keep the six sheets together.

4. Take the pan off the heat. Unwrap the pastry. Cut all the sheets into six squares. Cover them with foodwrap.

Use a pastry brush.

5. Put the butter in a small pan and melt it over a low heat. Brush a little butter over one of the pastry squares.

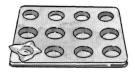

6. Put the square into a hole in the tray, buttered side up. Press it gently into the hole. Brush butter onto another square.

Overlap the pastry sheets so that they look like a star.

7. Put this square over the first one. Overlap the corners slightly. Butter and add a third square. Repeat in all the holes.

8. Put the tray on the middle shelf of the oven and cook for 10 minutes. Take it out and leave it to cool for five minutes.

Heat the apples until they bubble a little.

9. Take the pastry cases out of the tray and put them onto a large plate. Heat the apples again for about two minutes.

Eat the pies warm or cold.

10. Spoon the apple mixture into the pastry cases, so that they are almost full. Sift icing sugar onto them.

Painted biscuits

To make about 15 biscuits, you will need:
50g (2oz) icing sugar
75g (3oz) soft margarine
the yolk from a large egg
vanilla essence
150g (5oz) plain flour
plastic foodwrap
big cutters
a greased baking sheet

To decorate the biscuits:
an egg yolk
food dyes

Heat the oven to 180°C, 350°F,
gas mark 4, before you start.

Use a
wooden
spoon.

1. Sift the icing sugar through a sieve into a large bowl. Add the margarine and mix well until they are smooth.

2. Add the large egg yolk and stir it in well. Then, add a few drops of vanilla essence. Stir the vanilla into the mixture.

3. Hold a sieve over the bowl and pour the flour into it. Sift the flour through the sieve, to remove any lumps.

4. Mix in the flour until you get a smooth dough. Wrap the dough in plastic foodwrap and put it in the freezer.

Decorate your biscuits with lots of different patterns.

It takes time to decorate the biscuits, so you could freeze some of the dough to use another day.

5. Put the egg yolk into a bowl and beat it with a fork. Put it onto saucers. Mix a few drops of food dye into each one.

6. Take the dough out of the freezer. Roll out half of it onto a floury work surface, until it is as thin as your little finger.

7. Press out shapes with cutters. Use a fish slice to lift them onto a baking sheet. Roll out the rest of the dough.

8. Cut out more shapes. Use a clean paintbrush to paint shapes on the biscuits with the egg and dye mixture.

9. Bake the biscuits for 10-12 minutes. Remove them from the oven. Let them cool a little, then lift them onto a wire rack.

Starry jam tart

To make one jam tart, you will need:
350g (12oz) packet shortcrust pastry
about 2 tablespoons plain flour
6 rounded tablespoons seedless raspberry or
strawberry jam
1 tablespoon of milk
20cm (8in) fluted flan tin
a small star-shaped cutter

Heat the oven to 200°C, 400°F, gas mark 6, before you start.

You can use any
shape of cutter you
like. Stars and holly
leaves look very
Christmassy.

1. Take the pastry out of the fridge and leave it for 10 minutes. Sprinkle a clean work surface with some flour.

2. Cut off quarter of the pastry and wrap it in some plastic foodwrap. Sprinkle some flour onto a rolling pin.

Sift a slice of tart with a little icing sugar and serve it with cream.

The rolling pin cuts off the extra pastry.

3. Roll out the bigger piece of pastry. Turn it a little, then roll it again. Make a circle about 30cm (12in) across.

4. Put the rolling pin at one side of the pastry. Roll the pastry around it and lift it up. Place it over the tin and unroll it.

5. Dip a finger into some flour and press the pastry into the edges of the tin. Then, roll the rolling pin across the top.

6. Spoon the jam into the pastry case. Spread it out with the back of a spoon. Roll out the other quarter of the pastry.

7. Using the cutter, cut out about 12 pastry shapes. Brush them with a little milk and place them on top of the jam.

The pastry should be golden brown.

8. Put the jam tart in the oven. Bake it for about 20 minutes. Take the tart from the oven and let the jam cool before serving.

Peppermint creams

To make about 25 peppermint creams, you will need:
250g (9oz) icing sugar
half the white of a small egg, mixed from dried
egg white (mix as directed on the packet)
1 teaspoon peppermint flavouring
2 teaspoons lemon juice
green food dye
a rolling pin
small cutters
a baking sheet covered in
plastic foodwrap

Put peppermint
creams in boxes, to
give as presents.

1. Sift the icing sugar through a sieve into a large bowl. Make a hole in the middle of the sugar with a spoon.

2. Mix the egg white, peppermint flavouring and lemon juice in a small bowl. Pour the mixture into the sugar.

3. Use a blunt knife to stir the mixture. Then, squeeze it between your fingers until it is smooth, like a dough.

4. Cut the mixture into two pieces. Put each piece into a bowl. Add a few drops of green food dye to one bowl.

5. Use your fingers to mix in the dye. If the mixture is sticky, add a little more icing sugar and mix it in.

6. Sprinkle a little icing sugar onto a clean work surface. Sprinkle some onto a rolling pin too, to stop the mixture sticking

Cut the shapes close together

7. Roll out the green mixture until it is about as thick as your little finger. Use cutters to cut out lots of shapes.

8. Use a blunt knife to lift the shapes onto the baking sheet. Roll out the white mixture and cut out more shapes.

9. Lift all the shapes onto the baking sheet. Leave them for at least an hour until they become hard.

Shortbread

To make eight pieces, you will need:
butter for greasing
150g (5oz) plain flour
25g (1oz) rice flour or ground rice
100g (4oz) butter, refrigerated, cut into chunks
50g (2oz) caster sugar
a 20cm (8in) shallow round tin

Heat the oven to 150°C, 300°F, gas mark 2, before you start.

1. Grease the bottom and sides of the tin with some butter on a piece of paper towel. Make sure it is all greased.

2. Sift the flour and rice flour or ground rice through a sieve into a large bowl. Add the butter to the bowl.

3. Mix in the butter so that it is coated in flour. Rub it into the flour with your fingers until it is like fine breadcrumbs.

4. Stir in the sugar with a wooden spoon. Hold the bowl with one hand and squeeze the mixture into a ball with the other.

5. Press the mixture into the tin with your fingers. Use the back of a spoon to smooth the top and make it level.

6. Use a fork to press patterns around the edge and holes in the middle. Cut the shortbread into eight pieces.

Shortbread makes an ideal present.
See pages 62-63 for wrapping ideas.

7. Bake the shortbread for 30 minutes, until it is golden. After 10 minutes, take it out of the tin. Put it on a wire rack to cool.

Fairy muffins

To make 10 muffins, you will need:

300g (10oz) plain flour
2 teaspoons baking powder
150g (5oz) caster sugar
1 lemon
50g (2oz) butter
225ml (8 fl oz) milk
1 medium egg
100g (4oz) seedless raspberry jam
a 12-hole muffin tin
small sweets and sugar strands, for
    decorating

For the icing:
175g (6oz) icing sugar
2 tablespoons lemon juice squeezed from
    the lemon from the main mixture

Heat your oven to 200°C, 400°F, gas mark
6, before you start.

✿ The muffins need to be stored in an airtight container
and should be eaten on the day you make them.

Use a pastry brush.

If you are having
a party, you could
decorate some of
the muffins with
little candles.

1. Brush oil in ten of the
muffin holes. Then, cut a
small circle of baking
parchment to put in the
bottom of each hole.

2. Sift flour and baking
powder into a large bowl.
Add caster sugar, then
mix everything together
with a metal spoon.

Use a lemon
squeezer.

Heat the
pan gently.

3. Grate the rind from the lemon using the medium holes on a grater. Then, cut the lemon in half and squeeze the juice from it.

4. Put two tablespoons of juice on one side, for the icing. Then, cut the butter into pieces and put it in a pan with the lemon rind.

5. Add four tablespoons of milk and heat the pan until the butter melts. Take it off the heat and add the rest of the milk.

6. Break the egg into a cup and mix well with a fork, then stir it into the butter mixture. Add the mixture to the bowl.

7. Stir everything together with a fork. Then, nearly fill each muffin hole with the mixture and bake the muffins for 15 minutes.

8. Leave the muffins in the tin for three minutes, then loosen them with a blunt knife. Put them on a wire rack to cool.

Use a sharp knife.

9. Turn each muffin on its side and cut it in half. Then, spread jam on the bottom half and lay the top half on top.

10. Sift the icing sugar into a bowl and mix in lemon juice. Spoon icing onto the muffins and press on some sweets.

Shining star biscuits

To make about 20 biscuits, you will need:
50g (2oz) light soft brown sugar
50g (2oz) butter, softened
a small egg
115g (4½oz) plain flour
15g (½oz) cornflour
1 teaspoon ground mixed spice
solid boiled sweets
a large star-shaped cutter
a fat drinking straw
a small round cutter, slightly bigger than the sweets
a large baking tray lined with baking parchment

Heat the oven to 180°C, 350°F, gas mark 4, before you start.

Thread thin ribbon through the holes.

1. Using a wooden spoon, mix the sugar and butter really well, getting rid of any lumps in the mixture.

2. Break the egg into a separate bowl. Beat the egg with a fork until the yolk and the white are mixed together.

3. Mix half of the beaten egg into the mixture in the bowl, a little at a time. You don't need the other half.

4. Sift the flour, cornflour and mixed spice through a sieve. Mix everything together really well with a wooden spoon.

5. Squeeze the mixture with your hands until a firm dough is formed. Make the dough into a large ball.

6. Sprinkle a clean work surface with a little flour. Then, roll out the ball of dough until it is 5mm (¼in) thick.

If you hang biscuits on a Christmas tree, don't eat them afterwards.

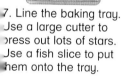

7. Line the baking tray. Use a large cutter to press out lots of stars. Use a fish slice to put them onto the tray.

8. Make a hole in each star by pressing the straw through the dough, near to the top of one of the points.

9. Use a small round cutter to cut a hole in the middle of each star. The hole should be slightly bigger than the sweet.

10. Squeeze the leftover pieces of dough into a ball. Roll them out. Cut out more stars. Put them on the baking tray.

11. Drop a sweet into the hole in the middle of each star shape. Put the baking tray on the middle shelf of the oven.

12. Bake the shapes for twelve minutes, then take them out. Leave them on the baking tray until they are cold.

Snowmen and presents

To make lots of snowmen and presents, you will need:
250g (9oz) 'white' marzipan*
green, red and yellow food dyes
toothpicks

Colouring marzipan

Add a little icing sugar if the marzipan gets too sticky.

1. Unwrap the marzipan. Then, put it on a plate and cut it into quarters. Put each quarter into a small bowl.

2. Add one drop of green food dye, then mix it in with your fingers. Carry on until the marzipan is evenly coloured.

3. Leave one quarter of the marzipan 'white'. Add red food dye to one quarter, and yellow to the other. Mix in the dye.

A snowman

Put the marzipan balls on a plate.

Press the ball with your thumb.

Cross the ends of the scarf.

1. Roll a piece of 'white' marzipan into a ball. Then, make a smaller ball. Press the smaller ball onto the larger one.

2. Roll a small ball of red marzipan. Press it to make a circle. Put it on the snowman's head. Put a tiny red ball on top.

3. Roll a thin sausage from red marzipan. Wrap it around the snowman for a scarf. Press in a face with a toothpick.

* Marzipan contains ground nuts. Don't make these if you are allergic to nuts.

Ice a cake with butter icing (see pages 34-35) and decorate it with snowmen and presents.

A present

1. Roll a ball of red marzipan and put it on a work surface. Gently press the flat side of a knife down on the ball.

2. Turn the ball on its side and press it with the knife again. Keep on doing this until the ball becomes a cube.

3. Roll thin sausages of green marzipan. Press them onto the cube, in a cross. Add two loops in the middle for a bow.

Iced gingerbread hearts

To make about 20 biscuits, you will need:
350g (12oz) plain flour
2 teaspoons ground ginger
1 teaspoon of bicarbonate of soda
100g (4oz) butter or margarine, cut into chunks
175g (6oz) soft light brown sugar
1 medium egg
4 tablespoons golden syrup
white writing icing
silver cake-decorating balls
a large heart-shaped cutter
2 greased baking trays

Heat the oven to 190°C, 375°F, gas mark 5,
before you start.

You could wrap some
biscuits in tissue paper
or cellophane twists,
to give as a present.

1. Sift the flour, ground ginger and bicarbonate of soda into a large bowl. Add the butter or margarine chunks.

2. Rub the butter or margarine into the flour with your fingers until it is like fine breadcrumbs. Stir in the sugar.

3. Break the egg into a small bowl, then add the syrup. Beat well with a fork, then stir the egg mixture into the flour.

4. Mix with a metal spoon until you make a dough. Sprinkle flour onto a work surface. Put the dough on it.

5. Stretch the dough by pushing it away from you. Fold it in half and repeat. Carry on doing this until it is smooth.

6. Sprinkle more flour onto the work surface. Cut the dough in half. Roll out one half until it is 5mm (¼in) thick.

7. Use a cutter to cut out lots of hearts. Then, lift the hearts onto the greased baking trays with a fish slice.

8. Roll out the rest of the dough and cut out more hearts. Put them on the baking trays, then put the baking trays in the oven.

9. Bake the biscuits for 12-15 minutes. They will turn golden brown. Carefully lift the baking trays from the oven.

10. Leave the biscuits on the trays for about 5 minutes. Then, lift them onto a wire rack. Leave them to cool.

11. When the biscuits are cold, draw lines across them with the icing. Cross some of the lines over each other.

12. Leave the icing to harden a little. Then, push in a silver cake-decorating ball where the lines of icing cross.

Christmas tree cakes

To make 15 cakes, you will need:
100g (4oz) self-raising flour
2 medium eggs
100g (4oz) soft margarine
100g (4oz) caster sugar
paper cake cases
2 baking trays with shallow pans
small sweets for decorating

For the butter icing:
75g (3oz) butter or margarine, softened
175g (6oz) icing sugar, sifted
2 teaspoons lemon juice or a few
drops of vanilla essence

Heat the oven to 190°C, 375°F, gas mark 5,
before you start.

1. Break the eggs into a cup. Then, sift the flour through a sieve into a big bowl. Add the eggs, margarine and sugar.

2. Stir everything together with a wooden spoon. Carry on until you get a smooth creamy mixture.

3. Put the paper cases into the pans in the baking trays. Use a spoon to half-fill each case with the mixture.

Stir it very quickly.

4. Bake the cakes for about 20 minutes and carefully take them out of the oven. Leave them on a rack to cool.

5. To make the icing, put the butter or margarine into a bowl and stir it with a fork. Carry on until it is really creamy.

6. Add some of the icing sugar to the butter and stir it in. Mix in the rest of the icing sugar, a little at a time.

7. Stir the lemon juice or vanilla essence into the mixture. Add a little more if the icing is very thick.

Arrange the cakes into a tree shape, like this.

8. Spread some butter icing on the top of each cake. Use the sweets to make different patterns on each cake.

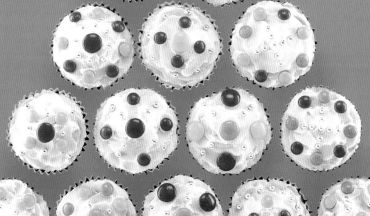

Use a flaky chocolate bar as a tree trunk.

Wrapping ideas

Tissue twists

1. Cut a square of tissue paper or thin cellophane. Then, put five or six biscuits in the middle of the square.

2. Gather up the edges of the square. Tie a piece of parcel ribbon around the tissue or cellophane, above the gift.

3. Decorate the wrapping with small stickers. You could also try wrapping biscuits with two colours of tissue or cellophane.

Wrapping sweets

Gift boxes filled with sweets and biscuits make great presents.

1. Cut a square of thin cellophane that is bigger than the sweet, like this. Put the sweet in the middle of the square.

Use a tiny piece of tape.

2. Wrap the sweet in the cellophane and tape it. Tie pieces of ribbon around each end of the sweet.

Gift boxes

Paint the inside of a gift box silver or gold. When the paint is dry, fill the box with lots of shredded tissue paper.

Lay a piece of ribbon across the lid and tape it inside. Lay another piece across it. Decorate the lid with stickers.

Cut a piece of tissue paper that is a little bigger than the box. Cut pieces in other colours. Line the box.

Find out how to make gift tags on page 64.

Tags and ribbons

A gift tag

1. Draw a holly leaf shape with a white wax crayon or white candle. Brush bright paint all over the card.

2. Carefully cut around the shape. Write a message on the back. Tape the end of the tag to a present.

Ribbon curls

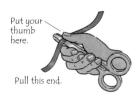

Put your thumb here.

Pull this end.

1. Cut a piece of parcel ribbon 25cm (10in) long. Cut more pieces the same length.

2. Hold a piece of ribbon between your thumb and the blade of some closed scissors. Pull it firmly.

3. The ribbon curls up. Curl the other pieces of ribbon. Tape them to the middle of a box.

DELICIOUS TREATS FOR EASTER

66 Chirpy chick cakes
68 Flower sweets
70 Sticky Easter cakes
72 Sunshine toast
74 Easter truffles
76 Marzipan animals and eggs
78 Flowery cut-out biscuits
80 Coloured eggs

82 Easter cake
84 Chocolate nests
86 Easter fruit bread
88 Spiced Easter biscuits
90 Easter daisy biscuits
92 Cheesy chicks
94 Gift-wrapping ideas
96 Easter gift tags

Chirpy chick cakes

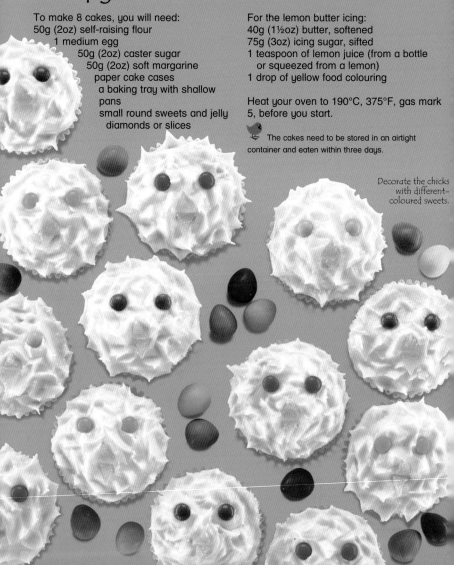

To make 8 cakes, you will need:
50g (2oz) self-raising flour
1 medium egg
50g (2oz) caster sugar
50g (2oz) soft margarine
paper cake cases
a baking tray with shallow pans
small round sweets and jelly diamonds or slices

For the lemon butter icing:
40g (1½oz) butter, softened
75g (3oz) icing sugar, sifted
1 teaspoon of lemon juice (from a bottle or squeezed from a lemon)
1 drop of yellow food colouring

Heat your oven to 190°C, 375°F, gas mark 5, before you start.

The cakes need to be stored in an airtight container and eaten within three days.

Decorate the chicks with different-coloured sweets.

1. Sift the flour through a sieve into a bowl. Break the egg into a cup, then add it to the flour. Add the sugar and margarine.

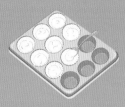

2. Beat the mixture firmly with a wooden spoon, until it is light and fluffy. Put eight paper cases into pans in the baking tray.

3. Using a teaspoon, half fill each paper case with the mixture. Then, bake the cakes in the oven for 18-20 minutes.

Bake the cakes until they are golden brown.

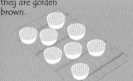

4. Take the cakes out of the oven. After a few minutes, lift them out of the baking tray and put them on a rack to cool.

5. For the icing, put the butter into a bowl. Beat it with a wooden spoon until it is creamy. Stir in half of the icing sugar.

6. Add the lemon juice, yellow food colouring and the rest of the icing sugar. Mix everything together well.

7. Using a blunt knife, cover the top of each cake with butter icing. Then, use a fork to make the icing look feathery.

8. Press two small round sweets onto each cake for the eyes. Then, cut eight of the jelly shapes in half for the beaks.

9. Press two halves into the icing on each cake, to make a beak. Make the pointed ends of the halves stick up a little.

Flower sweets

To make about 40 flowers,
you will need:

225g (8oz) icing sugar
1 tablespoon of lemon juice
   (from a bottle or squeezed
   from a lemon)
2 teaspoons egg white, mixed
   from dried egg white (mix
   as directed on the packet)
2-3 drops of lemon essence
small jelly sweets
a small flower-shaped cutter
a baking sheet

The flower sweets need to be
stored in an airtight container, on
layers of greaseproof paper. Eat
them within a week.

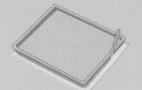

1. Put the baking sheet
on a piece of greaseproof
paper. Draw around the
tin and cut out the shape.
Put the shape in the tin.

2. Sift the icing sugar
through a sieve into a
large bowl. Make a hole
in the middle of the icing
sugar with a spoon.

*If the mixture is a little
dry, add a drop of water.*

3. Mix lemon juice, egg
white and lemon essence
in a small bowl. Pour into
the hole in the sugar.
Stir with a blunt knife.

4. Keep stirring until the
mixture starts to make a
ball. Then, squeeze it
between your fingers
until it is smooth.

5. Sprinkle a little icing
sugar onto a clean work
surface. Sprinkle some
onto a rolling pin too, to
stop the mixture sticking.

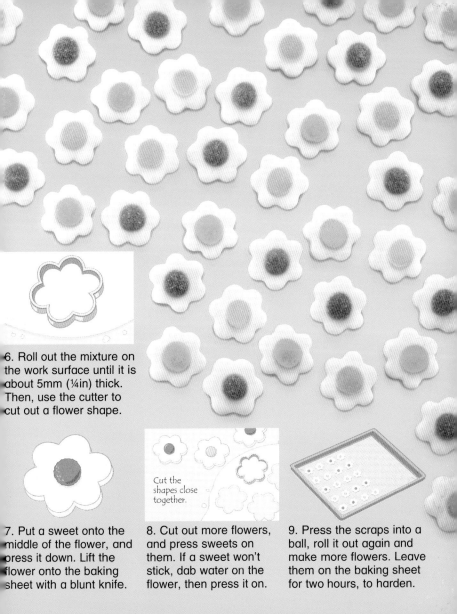

6. Roll out the mixture on the work surface until it is about 5mm (¼in) thick. Then, use the cutter to cut out a flower shape.

Cut the shapes close together.

7. Put a sweet onto the middle of the flower, and press it down. Lift the flower onto the baking sheet with a blunt knife.

8. Cut out more flowers, and press sweets on them. If a sweet won't stick, dab water on the flower, then press it on.

9. Press the scraps into a ball, roll it out again and make more flowers. Leave them on the baking sheet for two hours, to harden.

Sticky Easter cakes

This recipe is based on cakes that are traditionally eaten in Greece at Easter.

To make eight cakes, you will need:
100g (4oz) soft light brown sugar
100g (4oz) butter, softened
2 medium eggs
2 teaspoons baking powder
100g (4oz) semolina
½ teaspoon of ground cinnamon
100g (4oz) ground almonds*
4 tablespoons lemon juice (from a bottle or squeezed from a lemon)
a 12-hole muffin tin

For the orange and lemon syrup:
1 small orange
1 tablespoon of lemon juice (from a bottle or squeezed from a lemon)
4 tablespoons golden syrup

Heat your oven to 200°C, 400°F, gas mark 6, before you start.

🐤 The cakes need to be stored in an airtight container and eaten within three days. Don't pour the syrup over them more than two hours before serving.

You could serve the cakes with Greek yogurt and fresh orange segments.

Use a pastry brush.

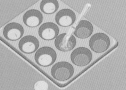

1. Brush some oil inside eight of the muffin holes. Cut a small circle of baking parchment to put in the bottom of each.

2. Put the sugar and the butter into a large bowl. Beat them together until they are mixed well and look creamy.

* Don't give these to anyone who is allergic to nuts.

3. Break the eggs into a small bowl and beat them. Stir in the beaten eggs, a little at a time, to the creamy mixture.

4. Mix the baking powder, semolina, cinnamon and almonds in a large bowl. Add them, and the lemon juice, to the mixture.

5. Mix everything well, then spoon the mixture into the holes in the tin. Bake the cakes in the oven for about 15 minutes.

The tin will
still be hot.

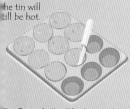

6. Carefully lift the cakes out of the oven. Leave them in the tin for a minute, then loosen their sides with a blunt knife.

7. Turn the cakes onto a large plate to cool. Then, carefully peel the baking parchment circles off each one.

8. For the syrup, grate some rind from about half of the orange on the fine holes on a grater. Put the rind into a small pan.

9. Cut the orange in half. Squeeze out the juice, using a lemon squeezer, and add 2 tablespoons of the juice to the pan.

10. Add the lemon juice and golden syrup. Over a very low heat, gently warm the mixture, stirring it all the time.

11. When the mixture is runny, use a teaspoon to trickle it over the cakes. Let the mixture cool a little before serving.

Sunshine toast

You will need:

margarine
1 slice of bread
1 small or medium egg
a large cookie cutter
a baking sheet

Heat your oven to
200°C, 400°F, gas
mark 6, before you
start.

The toast needs to
be eaten as soon as it's
cooked.

1. Dip a paper towel into some margarine. Then, rub the margarine all over the baking sheet, to grease it.

2. Using a knife, spread margarine on one side of the slice of bread. Then, press the cutter into the middle of the bread.

3. Lift out the shape you have cut out. Put both pieces of bread onto the baking sheet, with their margarine sides upwards.

You can use any cutter that makes a hole that is big enough to put an egg in.

4. Break the egg onto a saucer. Then, carefully slide the egg into the hole in the bread. Put the baking sheet in the oven.

5. Bake the bread and egg in the oven for seven minutes. Bake it for a little longer if you don't like a runny egg yolk.

6. Wearing oven gloves, carefully lift the baking sheet out of the oven. Use a fish slice to lift the pieces of toast onto a plate.

Easter truffles

To make 12 truffles, you will need:

225g (8oz) white, milk or plain chocolate drops
4 tablespoons double cream
1 teaspoon of vanilla essence
about 4 tablespoons sugar strands
small paper cases

The truffles need to be stored in an airtight container in a fridge. Eat them within five days.

1. Pour about 3cm (1in) of water into a pan. Heat the pan until the water bubbles, then remove the pan from the heat.

Wear oven gloves.

2. Put the chocolate drops and cream into a heatproof bowl. Using oven gloves, carefully put the bowl into the pan.

3. Stir the chocolate and cream with a wooden spoon until the chocolate has melted. Carefully lift the bowl out of the water.

4. Leave the bowl to cool for 20 minutes, then stir in the vanilla. Put the mixture in a fridge for 1½ hours, until it is very firm.

5. Put the sugar strands onto a plate. Scoop up some chocolate mixture with a teaspoon and put it into the sugar strands.

6. Using your fingers, roll the spoonful in the strands to make a ball. When it is covered, put it in a paper case.

7. Make more truffles. Put them on a plate in the fridge for 30 minutes, until they are hard. Keep them in the fridge.

To make truffle eggs, squash the spoonful of mixture slightly when you roll it in the sugar strands.

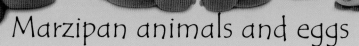

Marzipan animals and eggs

To make 4 chicks, 3 rabbits and lots of eggs and carrots, you will need:

250g (9oz) pack of marzipan*
yellow and red food colouring
toothpicks

 The animals and eggs need to be stored in an airtight container and eaten within three weeks.

Chicks

Wrap one half in plastic foodwrap.

1. Unwrap the marzipan and cut it in half. Put one half in a small bowl and add 12 drops of yellow food colouring.

2. Mix the colouring in with your fingers until the marzipan is completely yellow. Cut the piece of marzipan in half.

3. Put one half in a bowl and mix in a drop of red colouring. If the marzipan isn't bright orange, add another drop of red.

Keep this piece for the wings.

Press in two eyes with a toothpick.

4. Cut the yellow marzipan into five pieces. Make four of them into balls. Squeeze them at one end to make tear shapes.

5. Make eight small yellow wings and press two onto each body. Roll a beak from orange marzipan and press it on.

6. For the feet, make a tiny orange ball and flatten it. Cut the shape halfway across and open it out. Press a chick on top.

* Marzipan contains ground nuts, so don't give these to anyone who is allergic to nuts.

Rabbits

Use plastic foodwrap.

1. Unwrap the plain marzipan. Mix one drop of red colouring into it to make pink. Cut it in half and wrap one half.

2. Cut the unwrapped piece in half. With one half, make three balls, for the bodies. Then, cut the other piece in half.

3. From one half, roll three smaller balls, for the heads. Then, make six ears, three tails and three noses from the other half.

If the ears won't stick, dip the ends in water.

4. Pinch each ear to make a fold. Press ears, a head, nose and tail onto each body. Then, press in eyes with a toothpick.

Marbled eggs

1. Unwrap the second piece of pink marzipan. Add a drop of red colouring, and start to mix it in with your hands.

2. Stop mixing in the colouring when the marzipan looks marbled. Roll the marzipan into lots of little egg shapes.

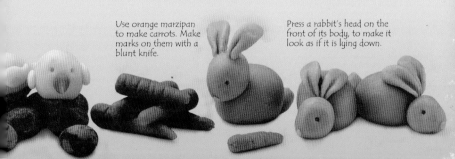

Use orange marzipan to make carrots. Make marks on them with a blunt knife.

Press a rabbit's head on the front of its body, to make it look as if it is lying down.

Flowery cut-out biscuits

To make about 10 biscuits, you will need:

100g (4oz) butter, softened
50g (2oz) caster sugar
a small orange
1 medium egg
2 tablespoons ground almonds*
200g (7oz) plain flour

1 tablespoon of cornflour
8 tablespoons seedless
   raspberry jam
a 5cm (2in) round cutter
a small flower cutter
2 greased baking trays

Heat your oven to 180°C, 350°F, gas mark 4, before you start.

✿ The biscuits need to be eaten on the day you make them.

* Don't give these biscuits to anyone who is allergic to nuts.

1. Put the butter and sugar into a large bowl. Mix them together with a wooden spoon until the mixture looks creamy.

2. Grate the rind from the orange using the medium holes on a grater. Add the rind to the bowl and stir it in.

3. Break the egg into a cup and mix it with a fork. Then, add a little of the egg to the creamy mixture and mix it in well.

4. Add some more egg to the bowl and mix it in. Carry on until you have added all the egg, then add the ground almonds.

5. Sift the flour and cornflour into the bowl. Then, mix everything with your hands until you have made a dough.

6. Wrap the dough in plastic foodwrap and put it in a fridge to chill for 30 minutes. While it is in there, heat your oven.

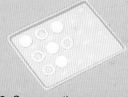

7. Sprinkle flour onto a clean work surface. Then, use a rolling pin to roll out the dough until it is about 3mm (⅛in) thick.

8. Using the round cutter, cut out lots of circles. Use the flower cutter to cut holes in the middle of half of the circles.

9. Squeeze the scraps into a ball. Then, roll out the ball and cut out more circles. Put all the circles on the baking trays.

The biscuits turn golden brown.

10. Bake the biscuits for 15 minutes. Leave on the baking trays for two minutes, then move onto a wire rack to cool.

11. Spread jam on the whole biscuits, as far as the edge. Then, place a flower biscuit on each one and press it down gently.

Coloured eggs

To make six coloured eggs, you will need:

6 eggs, at room temperature
food colouring
wax crayons
tiny star-shaped stickers
rubber bands

The eggs need to be stored in a fridge and eaten within three days. They can be eaten with a fresh mixed salad or on their own.

Cooking the eggs

Use a slotted spoon.

1. Put the eggs into a pan of cold water. Heat the pan until the water is gently boiling, then reduce the heat a little.

2. Cook the eggs for eight to nine minutes. Lift out one egg at a time. Cool them in a bowl of cold water for ten minutes.

Wax patterns

The wax resists the food colouring.

Leave the egg for about 10 minutes.

1. Using a wax crayon, draw patterns on a dry egg. Then, put 3-4 teaspoons of bright food colouring into a glass.

2. Half fill the glass with water, then put the egg into the glass. Using a spoon, turn the egg to colour it all over.

3. When the egg is brightly coloured, lift it out of the glass with a spoon. Carefully put the egg onto a paper towel to dry.

Stickers

Make sure the egg is dry.

1. Press tiny stickers onto an egg. Use shiny ones if you can, because they don't soak up so much food colouring.

2. Colour the egg in a glass, as you did before. Then, lift the egg out with a spoon and put it onto a paper towel to dry.

3. When the colouring is dry, peel off the stickers. You'll see the colour of the eggshell where the stickers were.

These rabbits and chicks were painted straight onto the eggs with food colouring.

Stripes

1. Stretch a short, thick rubber band around a dry egg. Then, stretch one around the egg from the top to the bottom.

2. Add lots more rubber bands, then colour the egg and let it dry. Then, remove the rubber bands to see stripes of eggshell.

81

Easter cake

You will need:

225g (8oz) self-raising flour
1 teaspoon of baking powder
4 medium eggs
225g (8oz) caster sugar
225g (8oz) soft margarine
two round 20cm (8in) cake tins

For the butter icing:
225g (8oz) icing sugar
100g (4oz) unsalted butter,
   softened
1 tablespoon of milk
1 teaspoon of vanilla essence

Heat your oven to 180°C, 350°F,
gas mark 4, before you start.

The cake needs to be stored in
an airtight container in a cool place
and eaten within three days.

To make the icing yellow,
add a teaspoon of
yellow food
colouring at
step 8.

Decorate the cake with
flower sweets (pages 68–
69) and marzipan chicks
(pages 76–77).

1. Put the cake tins onto a piece of greaseproof paper and draw around them. Cut out the circles, just inside the line.

2. Wipe the sides and bottoms of the tins with a little oil. Put the paper circles inside and wipe them with a little oil too.

3. Using a sieve, sift the flour and the baking powder into a large bowl. Then, carefully break the eggs into a cup.

4. Add the eggs, sugar and margarine to the bowl. Beat everything with a wooden spoon until they are mixed well.

5. Put half of the mixture into each tin. Smooth the tops with the back of a spoon. Then, bake the cakes for 25 minutes.

Be careful – the cakes will be hot.

6. Press the cakes with a finger. If they are cooked, they will spring back. Let them cool a little, then put them on a wire rack.

7. Peel the paper off the cakes and leave them to cool. When the cakes are cold, sift the icing sugar into a bowl.

8. Add the butter, milk and vanilla. Stir it all together, then beat until the mixture is fluffy. Put one cake on a plate.

9. Spread the cake with half of the icing. Then, put the other cake on top and spread it with the rest of the icing.

Chocolate nests

To make 10 nests, you will need:

225g (8oz) plain chocolate
50g (2oz) butter
2 tablespoons golden syrup
100g (4oz) corn flakes
30 chocolate mini eggs
paper cake cases
a baking tray with shallow pans

The nests need to be stored in an airtight container in a fridge. Eat them within three days.

1. Put ten paper cases into pans in the baking tray. Break the chocolate into squares and put them in a large pan.

84

The syrup slides off the hot spoon.

Try not to crush the flakes.

2. Add the butter to the pan. Dip a tablespoon in some hot water, then use the spoon to add the golden syrup.

3. Heat the pan gently, stirring the ingredients all the time, until the butter and chocolate have completely melted.

4. Turn off the heat, then add the corn flakes to the pan. Gently stir them into the chocolate, until they are coated all over.

Push the flakes up the sides.

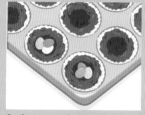

5. Fill the paper cases with the mixture. Using the back of a teaspoon, make a hollow in the middle of each nest.

6. Arrange three mini eggs in each nest. Then, put the tray in the fridge and leave it for about an hour to set.

7. Take the nests out of the paper cases and put them on a plate. Keep them in the fridge until you want to eat them.

Easter fruit bread

To make a loaf with about 12 slices, you will need:

225g (8oz) strong plain flour
½ teaspoon of ground mixed spice
½ teaspoon of salt
25g (1oz) butter
1 tablespoon of caster sugar
2 teaspoons easy-blend dried yeast
1 medium egg and 5 tablespoons milk, beaten together
100g (4oz) luxury dried mixed fruit
a little milk for brushing
a 20.5 x 12.5 x 8cm (8 x 5 x 3½in) loaf tin

For the icing:
50g (2oz) icing sugar
1 tablespoon of lemon juice (from a bottle or squeezed from a lemon)
50g (2oz) chopped glacé cherries

Heat your oven to 200°C, 400°F, gas mark 6.

🐤 Easter fruit bread needs to be stored in an airtight container and eaten within three days.

Draw around the bottom of the tin.

1. Put the tin onto baking parchment. Draw around it and cut out the shape. Grease the tin and put the paper in the bottom.

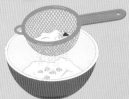

2. Sift the flour, mixed spice and salt through a sieve into a large bowl. Cut the butter into cubes and add it to the bowl.

3. Using your fingertips, rub in the butter until the mixture looks like breadcrumbs. Stir in the caster sugar and yeast.

Carry on until the dough is smooth and springy.

4. Pour the beaten egg mixture into the bowl. Stir everything together with a wooden spoon until you make a dough.

5. Sprinkle some flour onto a clean, dry work surface. Then, knead the dough by pushing it away from you with both hands.

6. Fold the dough in half and turn it around. Push it away again. Do this for five minutes, then put it into a greased bowl.

Knead in the fruit for a couple of minutes.

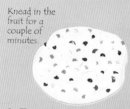

7. Cover the bowl with plastic foodwrap. Leave it in a warm place for an hour, until the dough has risen to twice its size.

8. Turn the dough out of the bowl and sprinkle the dried fruit over it. Knead the fruit into the dough until it is mixed in.

9. Put the dough in the tin and cover tin with plastic foodwrap. Put it in a warm place for about 45 minutes to rise some more.

Remove the baking parchment.

Use a teaspoon to drizzle the icing onto the loaf.

10. Heat your oven. Brush the top of the dough with milk, then put in the oven and bake the bread for 30-35 minutes.

11. Push a skewer into the loaf. If it comes out clean, the loaf is cooked. Take the loaf out of the tin. Put on a wire rack to cool.

12. Sift icing sugar into a bowl and mix in the lemon juice. Drizzle icing over the loaf, then scatter cherries on top.

Spiced Easter biscuits

To make about 25 biscuits, you will need:

1 medium egg
100g (4oz) butter, softened
75g (3oz) caster sugar
200g (7oz) plain flour
½ teaspoon of ground cinnamon
½ teaspoon of ground ginger
50g (2oz) currants
5 teaspoons milk
about 2 tablespoons
  caster sugar

a 6cm (2½in) fluted cookie
  cutter
two greased baking sheets

Heat your oven to 200°C,
400°F, gas mark 6.

The biscuits need to be stored
in an airtight container and eaten
within five days.

1. Carefully break the egg
on the edge of a small
bowl, and pour it slowly
onto a saucer. Then, put
an egg cup over the yolk.

You will use
the egg white
later.

2. Hold the egg cup
over the yolk and tip the
saucer over the small
bowl, so that the egg
white dribbles into it.

Use a wooden
spoon.

3. Put the butter and
sugar into a large bowl
and beat them until they
are creamy. Then, add the
egg yolk and beat it in.

Find out
how to make
cellophane
bags for your
biscuits on
page 95.

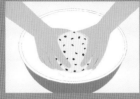

4. Using a sieve, sift the flour, the cinnamon and ginger into the bowl. Then, add the currants and the milk too.

5. Mix everything together with a spoon. Squeeze the mixture with your hands until you have made it into a dough.

6. Wrap the dough in plastic foodwrap. Put it in the fridge for 20 minutes. Then, sprinkle a clean work surface with flour.

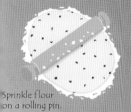

Sprinkle flour on a rolling pin.

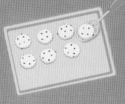

7. Heat your oven. Then, put the dough onto the work surface and roll it out until it is about 5mm (¼in) thick.

8. Use the cutter to cut out lots of biscuits. Then, carefully lift the biscuits onto the baking sheets, using a fish slice.

9. Squeeze the scraps of dough together to make a ball. Then, roll the dough out as you did before and cut out more biscuits.

Use a pastry brush.

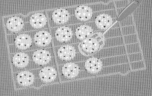

10. Using a fork, beat the egg white for a few seconds until it is frothy. Brush a little egg white on the top of each biscuit.

11. Sprinkle a little caster sugar over each biscuit. Bake them in the oven for 12-15 minutes. They will turn golden brown.

12. Leave the biscuits on the baking sheets for about five minutes. Then, lift them onto a wire rack and leave them to cool.

Easter daisy biscuits

To make about 30 biscuits, you will need:
75g (3oz) icing sugar
150g (5oz) butter, softened
a lemon
225g (8oz) plain flour
small sweets and silver cake-decorating balls
writing icing
a flower-shaped cookie cutter
two greased baking sheets

Heat your oven to 180°C, 350°F, gas mark 4.

The biscuits need to be stored in an airtight container and eaten within three days.

Use a sieve.

1. Sift the icing sugar into a large bowl. Add butter and mix everything with a spoon until the mixture is creamy.

2. Grate rind from the lemon using the medium holes on a grater. Add the rind to the bowl and mix everything again.

Use a lemon squeezer.

Sprinkle some flour on a rolling pin too.

3. Cut the lemon in half and squeeze the juice from it. Then, stir a tablespoon of lemon juice into the creamy mixture.

4. Sift the flour through a sieve into the bowl. Mix it in until you make a smooth dough. Wrap the dough in plastic foodwrap.

5. Put the dough in a fridge for 30 minutes, to become firmer. Then, sprinkle some flour onto a clean work surface.

6. Heat your oven. Then, roll out the dough until it is about 5mm (¼in) thick. Cut out lots of flower shapes, using the cutter.

The number of biscuits you make will depend on the size of your cutter.

7. Put the flower shapes onto the baking sheets. Squeeze the scraps into a ball, then roll out again and cut out more shapes.

The biscuits should be lightly browned.

8. Bake the biscuits for 15 minutes. Leave them on the baking sheets for two minutes, then put them on a wire rack to cool.

9. When the biscuits are cool, decorate with icing. Draw lines, swirls and dots. Press sweets into the middle of the icing.

Cheesy chicks

To make about 15 chicks, you will need:
75g (3oz) mature Cheddar cheese
100g (4oz) plain flour
50g (2oz) butter, refrigerated
the yolk from a medium egg
5 teaspoons cold water
a chick-shaped or other cookie
   cutter
two greased baking sheets

Heat your oven to 190°C,
375°F, gas mark 5.

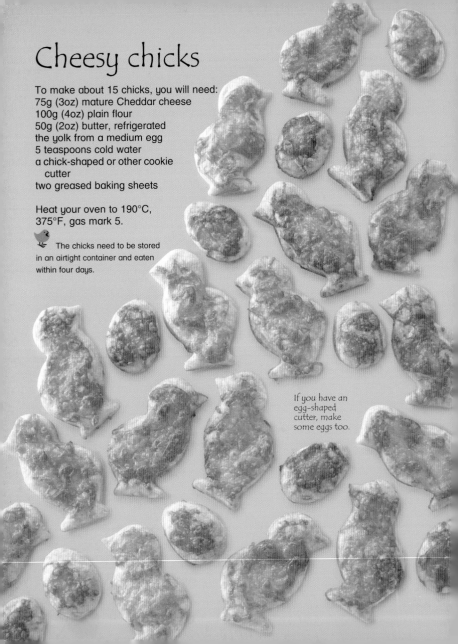 The chicks need to be stored
in an airtight container and eaten
within four days.

If you have an
egg-shaped
cutter, make
some eggs too.

Use the fine holes on a grater.

1. Grate the cheese. Sift the flour through a sieve into a large bowl. Then, cut the butter into chunks and add it to the bowl.

2. Mix in the butter until it is coated in flour. Rub it in with your fingers, until it looks like breadcrumbs. Add half of the cheese.

3. Mix the egg yolk and water in a small bowl. Put two teaspoonfuls in a cup, then pour the rest over the flour mixture.

4. Stir everything together, then squeeze the mixture until you make a smooth dough. Make it a slightly flattened round shape.

5. Wrap the dough in plastic foodwrap and put in a fridge to chill for 30 minutes. While it is in the fridge, heat your oven.

6. Sprinkle flour onto a clean work surface and a rolling pin. Roll out the dough until it is about 5mm (¼in) thick.

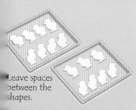

Leave spaces between the shapes.

Use a fish slice.

7. Use the cutter to cut out chick shapes. Put them onto baking sheets. Squeeze the scraps into a ball, then roll them out.

8. Cut out more shapes. Brush the tops of the shapes with the egg mixture, then sprinkle them with grated cheese.

9. Bake the chicks for 12 minutes. Leave them on the baking sheets for five minutes, then put them on a wire rack to cool.

Gift-wrapping ideas

Bunny boxes

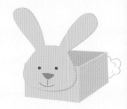

This side of the head needs to be on the fold.

1. Carefully cut the top off a tissue box and paint the box. Find a piece of thick paper the same colour and fold it in half.

2. Draw half of a bunny's head, like this. Keeping the paper folded, cut out the shape. Open out the paper and flatten it.

3. Draw a face. Glue the head onto one end of the box. Glue a piece of cotton wool onto the opposite end, for a tail.

Pretty sweets

1. Cut a square of thin cellophane that is bigger than the sweet, like this. Put the sweet in the middle of the square.

2. Wrap the cellophane around the sweet and tape it. Tie a piece of parcel ribbon around each end of the sweet.

Pile sweets or biscuits into a bunny box as an Easter gift.

Sweetie bags

Leave long ends on the ribbon.

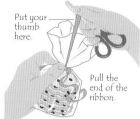

Put your thumb here.

Pull the end of the ribbon.

1. Cut a square of thin cellophane. Then, put several biscuits or some sweets in the middle of the square.

2. Gather up the edges of the square and tie a piece of parcel ribbon around the cellophane, above the biscuits.

3. To make the ribbon curl, hold it between your thumb and the blade of some closed scissors, and pull it firmly.

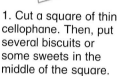

Add a paper handle to a box to make a basket.

Save food boxes and wrap ribbons around them.

Easter gift tags

1. Draw a rectangle on a piece of white card with a wax crayon. Then, draw the body of a chick with a yellow crayon.

Draw an egg shape and fill it with lines and patterns.

2. Add a beak, a leg and an eye. Paint over the picture with runny paint. The crayon lines will show through the paint.

You can fill different areas with different colours of paint, like this flower.

3. When the paint is dry, cut around the rectangle, leaving a painted edge. Tape a piece of ribbon to the back of the tag.

Managing designer: Mary Cartwright • Photographic manipulation: Emma Julings
Additional designs by Nicola Butler and Doriana Berkovic • With thanks to Katrina Fearn, Brian Voakes and Fiona Patchett
This edition first published in 2009 by Usborne Publishing Ltd., Usborne House, 83-85 Saffron Hill, London, England. www.usborne.com